# Mandala Me Inspirational Sayings
## Coloring Book for Kids, Teens and Adults

Color and relax coloring perfect creative designs!

by PK Burian

www.pkburian.com

ISBN-13 978-1535134361
ISBN-10 1535134364

# Introduction

Enter the world of creativity with Mandala Me Inspirational Saying Coloring Book. Inside you'll find 30 beautiful mandalas with original inspirational sayings. Enjoy your time patterning, shading, and coloring. Each detailed mandala will spark your imagination and unleash your artist inside. Printed on high-quality paper, this coloring book for kids, teens and adults is perfect for coloring with markers, colored pencils, or gel pens. Designed to eliminate bleed-through, each page may be removed and displayed.

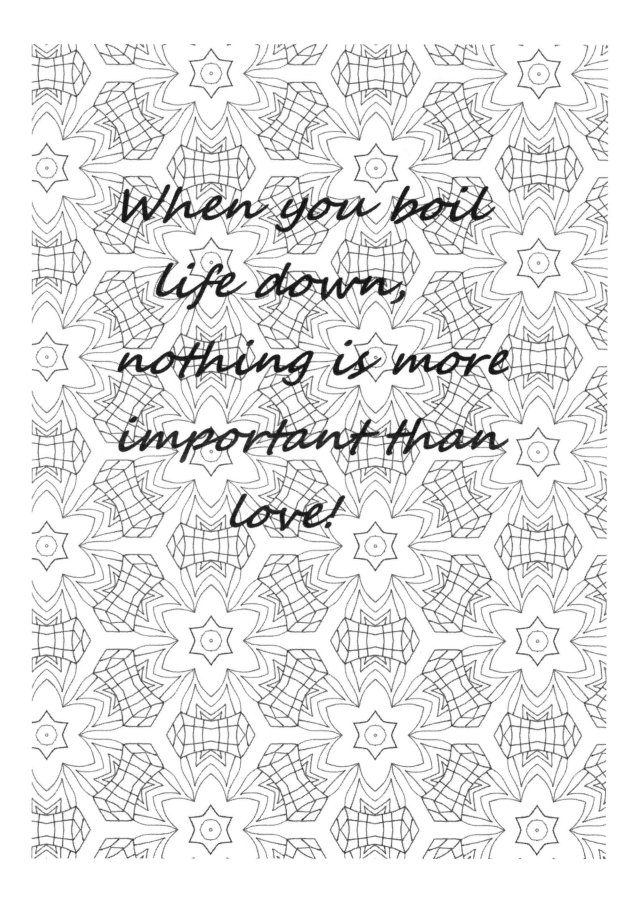

When you boil life down, nothing is more important than love!

We are today but a creation of what we have made from our past.

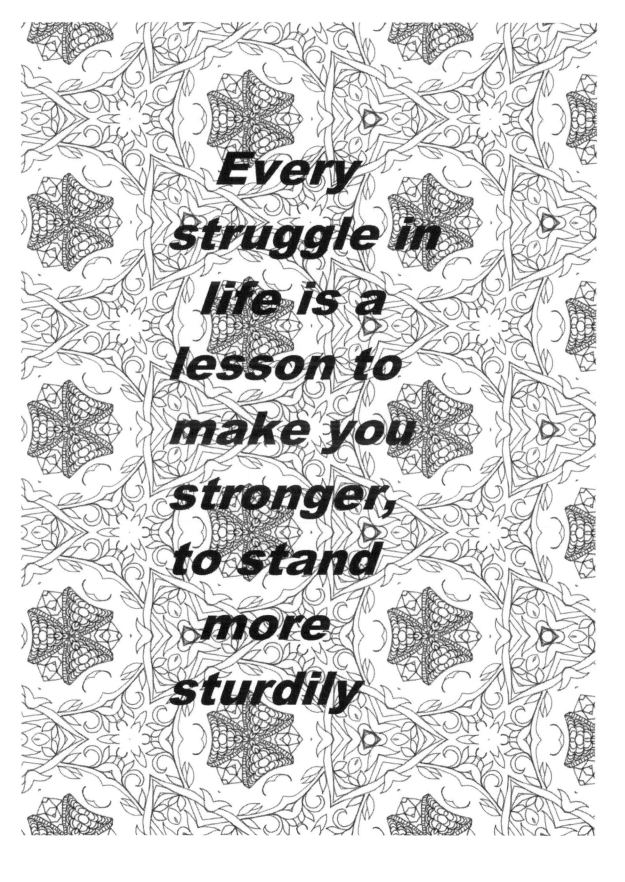

Every struggle in life is a lesson to make you stronger, to stand more sturdily

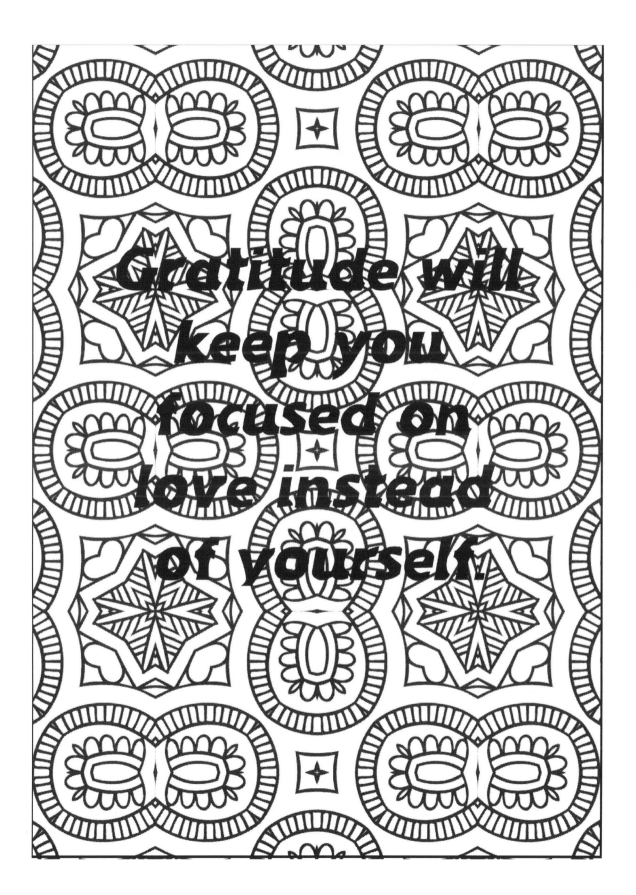

Gratitude will keep you focused on love instead of yourself.

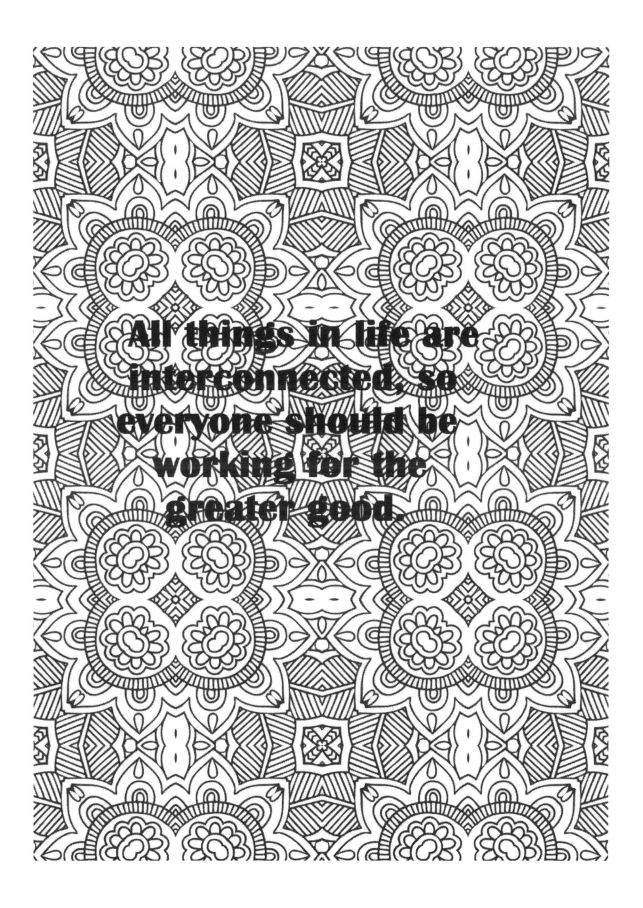

All things in life are interconnected, so everyone should be working for the greater good.

We are guided everyday in dreams, in writings, and in passing conversasitons. We just need to be aware of the message!

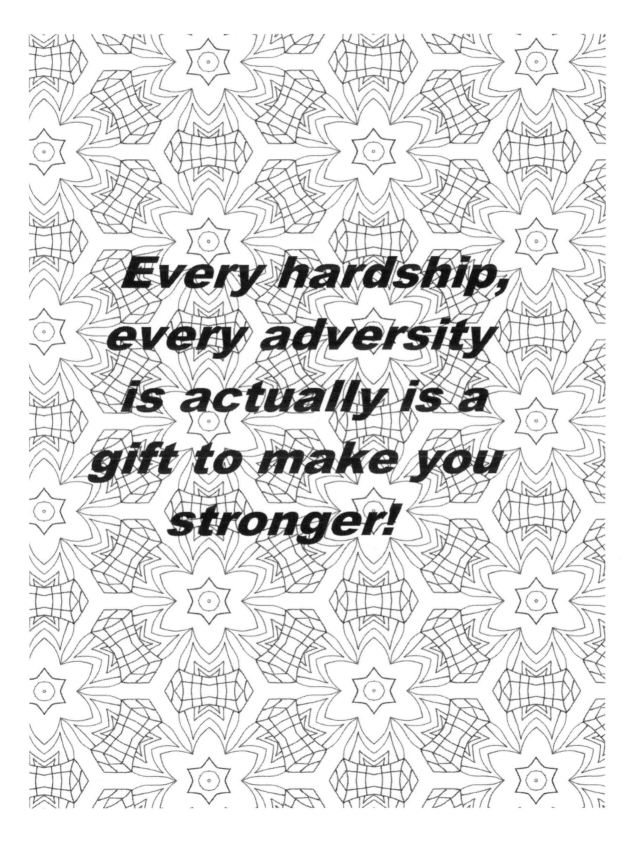

When things happen that are out of the ordinary, know there is an important lesson to learn

Each of us must earn his or her own way in life to keep growing!

Every Experience in life brings about a transformation within yourself

Because I listen,
I can hear my
inner guidance
speaking to me
about the
important
matters as well
as the smallest
things in my
life.

Look for good in everyone.

Love is not power.
Love is not control.
Love is not anger.
Love is the doorway
to heaven.

1. Imagine your goal clearly

2. Assume you already have it.

3. Surrender the outcome for the good of all.

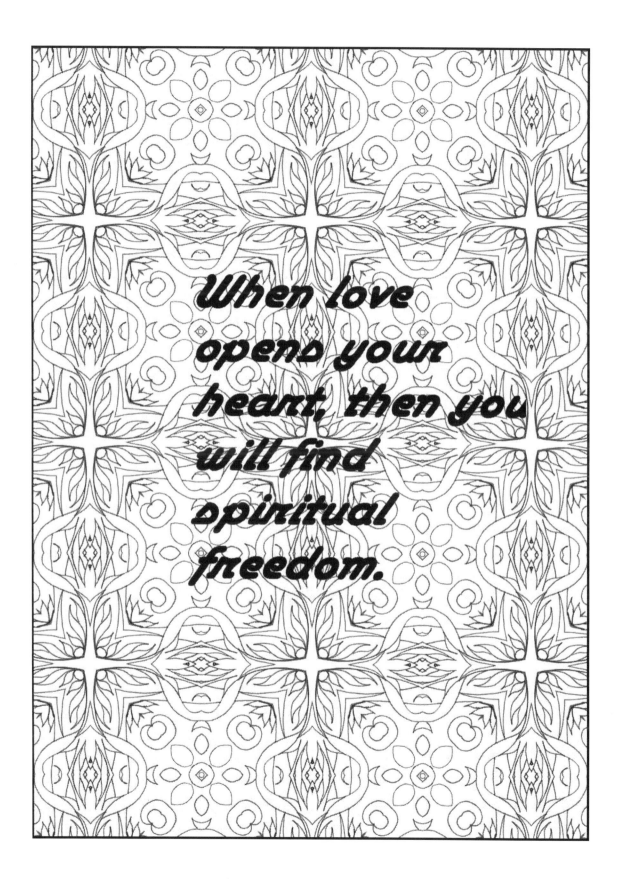

As changes occur in life,
be willing to surrender to
them. Know that every
experience in your life—
good and difficult—is a
gift.

Go to: **www.pkburian.com**

For more Mandala Me Coloring Books look on Amazon for:
Mandala Me Beautiful
Mandala Me Animals
Mandala Me Paisley
Mandala Me Paisley Pretty
Mandala Me Love
Mandala Me Hearts
Mandala Me A Holiday
Mandala Me Floral
Mandala Me Inspirational Sayings

And for kids:
Animals of the Forest
Bears, Bears, Bears Coloring Book
Bears, Bears, Bears Activity Book
Birds of a Feather
Butterflies Everywhere
Happy Farm Animals
My Favorite Pet
More coming soon!

.

Proof

Made in the USA
Charleston, SC
10 August 2016